I0821535

Smokey the Bear Sutra

And he will
protect
those who love
woods and *rivers*,
Gods and *animals*,
hobos and *madmen*,
prisoners and
sick people,
musicians,
playful women, and
hopeful children.

Gary Snyder

SMOKEY THE BEAR Sutra

Applewood Books
CARLISLE, MASSACHUSETTS

978-1-4290-9634-8

Smokey the Bear Sutra was written by poet Gary Snyder, an American Pulitzer Prize recipient, on a night in February of 1969 at a Sierra Club wilderness conference. He dedicated the poem to the public domain—free for all of us, forever.

Thank you for purchasing an Applewood book. Applewood reprints America's lively classics—books from the past that are still of interest to modern readers. Our mission is to build a picture of America's past through its primary sources.

To inquire about this edition or to request a free copy of our current catalog featuring our best-selling books, write to:

Applewood Books
P.O. Box 27
Carlisle, MA 01741

For more complete listings, visit us on the web at www.awb.com

10 9 8 7 6 5 4 3 2 1

PRINTED IN CHINA

The short works Applewood offers in its American Roots series have been selected to connect us. The books are tactile mementos of American passions by some of America's most famous writers. Each of these has meant something very personal to me.

Gary Snyder composed "Smokey the Bear Sutra" in one night at a Sierra Club conference in 1969. I had just started college in Colorado. I spent many of my free days in the early 1970s unsuccessfully fly-fishing in Colorado rivulets and mountain streams, surrounded by the numinous land. How it and all of us on it need a protector, and Snyder set out to create one that turned the Forest Service's Smokey Bear image on its head. The message of the sutra is that we as beings are responsible to protect all other life down to the smallest forms—do no harm, protect our collective selves, and honor the great impermanence.

> "*And he will protect those who love woods and rivers, Gods and animals, hobos and madmen, prisoners and sick people, musicians, playful women, and hopeful children.*"

Phil Zuckerman
PUBLISHER

Once in the Jurassic, about 150 million years ago, the Great Sun Buddha in this corner of the Infinite Void gave a great discourse to all the assembled elements and energies: to the standing beings, the walking beings, the flying beings, and the sitting beings—even grasses, to the number of thirteen billion, each one born from a seed, assembled there: a Discourse concerning

Enlightenment on the planet Earth.

"In some future time, there will be a continent called America. It will have great centers of power called such as Pyramid Lake, Walden Pond, Mt. Rainier, Big Sur, Everglades, and so forth; and powerful nerves and channels such as Columbia River, Mississippi River, and Grand Canyon. The human race in that era will get into troubles all over its head, and practically wreck everything in spite of its own strong intelligent Buddha-nature."

"The twisting strata of the

great mountains and the pulsings of volcanoes are my love burning deep in the earth. My obstinate compassion is schist and basalt and granite, to be mountains, to bring down the rain. In that future American Era I shall enter a new form: to cure the world of loveless knowledge that seeks with blind hunger; and mindless rage eating food that will not fill it."

AND HE SHOWED HIMSELF
IN HIS TRUE FORM OF
SMOKEY
THE BEAR

A handsome smokey-colored brown bear standing on his hind legs, showing that he is aroused and watchful.

Bearing in his right paw the Shovel that digs to the truth beneath appearances; cuts the roots of useless attachments, and flings damp sand on the fires of greed and war;

His left paw in the mudra of Comradely Display—indicating that all creatures have the full right to live to their limits and that deer, rabbits, chipmunks, snakes, dandelions, and lizards all grow in the realm of the Dharma;

Wearing the blue work overalls symbolic of slaves and laborers, the countless men oppressed by a civilization that claims to save but only destroys;

Wearing the broad-brimmed hat of the West, symbolic of the forces that guard the Wilderness, which is the Natural State of the Dharma and the True Path of man on earth:

all true paths lead through mountains—

With a halo of smoke and flame behind, the forest fires of the kali-yuga, fires caused by the

stupidity of those who think
things can be gained and lost
whereas in truth all is contained
vast and free in the Blue Sky and
Green Earth of One Mind;
  Round-bellied to show his
kind nature and that the great
Earth has food enough for every-
one who loves her and trusts her;
  Trampling underfoot wasteful
freeways and needless suburbs;
smashing the worms of capitalism
and totalitarianism;
  Indicating the Task: his
followers, becoming free of cars,
houses, canned foods, universities,
and shoes, master the Three

Mysteries of their own Body, Speech, and Mind; and fearlessly chop down the rotten trees and prune out the sick limbs of this country America and then burn the leftover trash.

Wrathful but (calm, Austere but Comic. Smokey the Bear will Illuminate those who would help him; but for those who would hinder or slander him)

HE WILL
PUT THEM OUT.

Thus his great Mantra:

Namah samanta vajranam
chanda maharoshana Sphataya
hum traka ham mam

"I DEDICATE
MYSELF TO THE
UNIVERSAL
DIAMOND BE THIS
RAGING FURY
DESTROYED"

And he will protect those
who love woods and rivers, Gods
and animals, hobos and madmen,
prisoners and sick people, musicians, playful women, and hopeful
children;

And if anyone is threatened by advertising, air pollution, or the police, they should chant *SMOKEY THE BEAR'S WAR SPELL:*

DROWN
THEIR BUTTS
CRUSH
THEIR BUTTS
DROWN
THEIR BUTTS
CRUSH
THEIR BUTTS

And SMOKEY THE BEAR will surely appear to put the

enemy out with his vajra-shovel.
Now those who recite this
Sutra and then try to put it in
practice will accumulate merit

as countless as the sands of
Arizona and Nevada,

Will help save the planet Earth
from total oil slick,

Will enter the age of harmony
of man and nature,

Will win the tender love and
caresses of men, women, and
beasts,

Will always have ripe blackberries to eat and a sunny spot under a pine tree to sit at.

AND IN THE END
WILL WIN
HIGHEST PERFECT
ENLIGHTENMENT

...thus we have heard...

(may be reproduced free forever)